For my siblings: Lee Lee/Sarah & Michael/Sike, and all
the games we played (from Maria/Jessica) —M.G.

For my wonderful family and friends —M.P.

Millbrook Press™
An imprint of Lerner Publishing Group, Inc.
241 First Avenue North
Minneapolis, MN 55401 USA

For reading levels and more information, look up this title at www.lernerbooks.com.

Designed by Emily Harris.
Main body text set in Mikado medium and Plumcake regular.
Typeface provided by HVD Fonts and Pintassilgoprints.
The illustrations in this book were created using paints, handmade textures, and
digital media.

Library of Congress Cataloging-in-Publication Data

Names: Gianferrari, Maria, author. | Powell, Mia, 1996– illustrator.
Title: Play like an animal! : why critters splash, race, twirl, and chase / Maria
    Gianferrari ; illustrated by Mia Powell.
Description: Minneapolis : Millbrook Press, [2020] | Audience: Age 5–9. |
    Audience: K to Grade 3. | Includes bibliographical references. | Identifiers: LCCN
    2019017412 (print) | LCCN 2019020619 (ebook) | ISBN 9781541583788 (eb pdf) |
    ISBN 9781541557710 (lb : alk. paper)
Subjects: LCSH: Play behavior in animals—Juvenile literature.
Classification: LCC QL763.5 (ebook) | LCC QL763.5 .G53 2020 (print) |
    DDC 591.56/3—dc23

LC record available at https://lccn.loc.gov/2019017412

Manufactured in the United States of America
1-46166-45960-8/14/2019

PLAY LIKE AN ANiMAL!

WHY CRITTERS SPLASH, RACE, TWIRL, AND CHASE

Maria Gianferrari

illustrated by **Mia Powell**

M Millbrook Press • Minneapolis

DASH!
HIDE!
SPLASH!
RIDE!

You love to play!
Animals do too!
When animals play, they're practicing how to

FIGHT,

GET ALONG,

HUNT,

MATE,

and ESCAPE FROM PREDATORS.

But most of all, they're having fun, just like you!

PLONK, DIG, SLIDE!

Collared peccaries play in the mud.

RUB, PLOP, BLOW!

Rhinos are mud splashers too.

Rhinos and peccaries wallow. Wallowing coats their skin with mud, which keeps them cool, repels insects, and protects their skin from sunburn.

RACE, HANG, CHASE!

Monkeys play in trees.

Playing in trees helps monkeys practice fleeing from predators and build strong muscles.

SLIP, SLIDE, SLED!

Ravens play in the snow.

Ravens and river otters are curious creatures. Exploring new areas and making new movements helps sharpen their problem-solving skills.

BELLY SLIDE,

FLIP,

GLIDE!

River otters romp on mud, snow, and ice.

VAULT, SURF, SOMERSAULT!

Dolphins play in the water.

SPLASH, DUNK, SWIM!

Elephants frolic in the water.

Dolphins and elephants are intelligent creatures who live together in groups. Playing together is good for cooperation.

PUNCH,

KICK,

SMACK-SLAP!

Kangaroos box.

Joeys box with their mothers, who let them win. When kangaroos play-fight, they're practicing how to defend themselves against predators.

NIBBLE-FUMBLE,
HURDLE-TUMBLE,
READY TO RUMBLE!

Rats wrestle.

Rat pups roll, chase, mount, pounce, and box. Wrestling teaches rats to play by the rules.

PULL, PUSH, YANK!

Wolves play tug-of-war.

When wolf pups and other canines play tug-of-war, they're learning how to practice fair play.

JUMP, WHIRL!

BOUND, TWIRL!

Ungulates love to leap!

An ungulate (UN-gyou-lit) is a mammal with hooves. When goats, horses, giraffes, and antelopes leap, they're improving their coordination, which can help them escape from predators.

SWAY, TAP . . . BOLT!

Gorillas play tag.

By playing tag, gorillas and other apes improve their communication skills, deal with conflicts better, and figure out what kind of behavior is acceptable.

DIP, DIVE! TOSS, CATCH!
TAKE, MAKE! CHUCKLE, CHORTLE!

Keas play in all kinds of ways!

Keas, a type of parrot from New Zealand, are smart and full of mischief. They play tag in the air and catch with rocks and sticks. Keas steal objects from yards and make their own toys, like sleds from doormats. They even laugh—they have a special play call that makes nearby keas join in the fun.

YOU . . .
PLONK AND PLOP!

RACE AND CHASE!

SLIDE AND GLIDE!

SURF AND SPLASH!

BOX-WRESTLE-TUG!

WHIRL AND TWIRL!

SWAY AND PLAY

LIKE AN ANIMAL!

WHY PLAY?

To stay healthy, doctors say, "Play every day!" Why? Because it's fun! And scientists say free play stimulates brain growth. That's just a fancy way of saying playing makes you smarter and more ready to face the world. Make time for play every day!

PLAY BY THE RULES, LIKE THESE ANIMALS DO!

If an animal is hurt during play, it steps away from the more aggressive friend.

The aggressor approaches the hurt friend to apologize.

The hurt friend accepts the apology, and the play begins again.

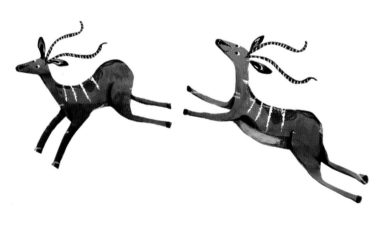

PLAY LIKE THESE ANIMALS . . .

Spring like a sifaka! Physical play makes you strong. Sifakas, a kind of lemur, have short arms, so they jump between tree branches.

Tumble and tag like a meerkat! Social play helps you cooperate with friends. Meerkats live in groups called mobs in underground burrows.

Experiment like an octopus! Imaginative play promotes creativity. Octopuses in captivity play catch with floating objects and explore puzzles, Legos, and other toys.

MORE FUN ANIMAL FACTS

COLLARED PECCARIES

Also known as javelinas, collared peccaries live in the deserts of the southwestern United States and the tropical rain forests of Central and South America. They live together in herds and eat a wide variety of foods: prickly pear cactus, roots, tubers and greens, lizards, rodents, and dead birds. They are like eco-engineers: the wallows they dig hold water for drinking and bathing and attract insects and frogs.

RHINOS

There are five species of rhinos. White and black rhinos live in the African grasslands. The grasslands and tropical rain forests of Asia are home to Javan, Sumatran, and Indian rhinoceroses. They graze on grasses, trees, and bushes. Some rhinos have two horns and some have only one horn, but all babies are born without horns.

MONKEYS

There are 260 species of monkeys, and they're grouped into Old World monkeys, which live in Africa and Asia, and New World monkeys, which live in the Americas. Only New World monkeys have prehensile tails—ones that can grasp. Many monkeys are arboreal, meaning they dwell in treetops. However, some monkeys are ground dwellers. Most monkeys eat fruit, nuts, seeds, and flowers. Some also eat birds' eggs, insects, spiders and lizards. A group of monkeys can be called a troop, tribe, carload, cartload, or barrel.

RAVENS

Common ravens are among the world's most intelligent tool-using birds. Their range extends through much of North America and into Central America, as well as Europe, Asia, and northern Africa. Ravens will eat just about anything, but they love meat—especially carrion (dead animals). Ravens often alert wolves to dead animals ravens can't eat with their beaks. Wolves start the meal, and ravens get the leftovers.

RIVER OTTERS

Members of the weasel family, North American river otters live in all kinds of watery habitats: rivers, swamps, lakes, and estuaries. River otters love to eat fish, but they also eat crustaceans, waterfowl, frogs, turtles, snakes, and all kinds of eggs; they also eat rodents and birds on land. River otters' powerful tails help propel them in the water. They also have special eyelids that help them see underwater and flaps on their ears and nose that close when they're swimming. Otters can also hold their breath underwater for eight minutes.

DOLPHINS

There are forty-two species of dolphins worldwide. The smallest dolphin, the Hector's dolphin, approximately 3 feet (1 m) and 100 pounds (45 kg), lives in the shallow waters off the coast of New Zealand. The orca, or killer whale, is the world's largest dolphin. It can be 32 feet (9.8 m) long—almost as long as a school bus and weigh up to 6 tons (5.4 t)—the weight of six small cars. Most dolphins eat fish, but orcas eat seals and sea lions. When you hear the word *dolphin*, you probably picture a bottlenose dolphin frolicking in the ocean. But there are freshwater dolphins too, such as the Amazon River dolphin, which is pink!

ELEPHANTS

Elephants are the largest land mammals on Earth. There are two main species, the African elephant, which lives in the grasslands and forests of Africa, and the Indian elephant, which lives in the grasslands and forests of Asia. African elephants are larger, have bigger ears, and more wrinkled skin. Both males and females have tusks. Indian elephants have smaller ears, and only some males have tusks. Their trunks are different too. African elephants have two fingerlike tips on the ends of their trunks, while Indian elephants have only one. Elephants eat vegetation such as grasses and woody plants including fruits and roots.

KANGAROOS

Kangaroos are found only in Australia and New Guinea. They feed on fruit, grasses, moss, flowers, and insects. The red kangaroo is the world's largest marsupial. Males can be almost 6 feet (1.8 m) tall. It can jump almost 10 feet (3 m) high and nearly 25 feet (7.6 m) long! They live in central Australia. The other three species are the eastern grey kangaroo (eastern Australia and Tasmania), the western grey kangaroo (southern Australia), and the antilopine kangaroo (northern Australia). Tree kangaroos live in the rain forests of New Guinea. When older kangaroos box with younger ones and let them win so they don't get hurt, it's called self-handicapping.

RATS

These amazing animals live on every continent in the world except Antarctica. Though they originated in Asia, rats traveled to the rest of the world as stowaways on ships. The two main species of rats are the black, or house, rat and the Norway, or brown, rat. Country rats tend to eat plants, fruit, and seeds, while city rats eat our leftovers: garbage and meat. When rats play, they rub their snouts on their friends' necks. When they fight, they bite one another's butts! Scientists have demonstrated that rats laugh when they're tickled. Their laugh is a high-pitched chirping sound that can't be heard with human ears.

WOLVES

Wolves live in a variety of habitats all over the world—in North America, Europe, Asia, and Africa. There are two species of wolves, the gray wolf and the red wolf. Wolves are social animals who live and hunt in packs. Wolves are primarily carnivores—meat eaters. They will hunt large hooved animals such as bison, elk and deer, and smaller mammals such as rabbits, hare, rodents, and birds. Some even eat fish.

Wolves and other canines ask their friends to play by crouching on their front legs with their rumps in the air, and a wagging tail. This is called the play bow. They also use the play bow to apologize when play gets too rough.

UNGULATES

The hooves of ungulates are a kind of toenail. There are even-toed ungulates: those with cloven (two-toed) hooves like goats, deer, or camels, or with four toes like hippos. Odd-toed ungulates have one toe, like a horse or zebra, or three toes like a tapir. Ungulates eat grasses, woody plants, and trees. When ungulates leap, they caper, which is a jump with a joyful, twisting-turning motion.

GORILLAS

Gorillas are members of the great ape family and the largest primates. They live in the tropical and subtropical rain forests of central Africa. There are two main species, the eastern gorilla and the western gorilla. Gorillas eat fruits, shoots, and stems. Some eat termites and ants too.

When gorillas want to play tag, they first ask their friends by making a play face. Try it! Open your mouth, but cover your top teeth with your lip. Only your bottom teeth should be showing. That's it! When gorillas gambol, they are strolling toward each other with a bouncy walk while swaying their shoulders and heads side to side.

KEAS

Keas live only on the South Island of New Zealand. They are nicknamed mountain monkeys and clowns of the Alps, both because of their intelligent, mischievous nature and because they are the world's only alpine parrot. Keas eat a wide variety of foods: insects and other invertebrates, roots, seeds, fruit, flowers, and nectar. They even eat other birds, chicks and eggs, and carrion too.

Because these clever birds kept moving highway cones and were being hit by cars, kea experts created a gym to keep them physically and intellectually stimulated. The gym has ladders, swings, floatation devices that spin, and climbing frames that are rearranged to keep the keas engaged.

FURTHER READING

Bekoff, Marc. *Animals at Play: Rules of the Game*. Philadelphia: Temple University Press, 2008.

Bingham, Caroline, and Fleur Star. *Animal Playtime*. New York: DK, 2011.

London, Jonathan. *Otters Love to Play*. Somerville, MA: Candlewick, 2016.

Neuman, Susan B. *Let's Play! Collection*. Washington, DC: National Geographic Kids, 2017.

Stefoff, Rebecca. *How Animals Play*. New York: Cavendish Square, 2014.